THE WORLD AROUND ME

T0005058

COLORS

··· IN MY WORLD ···

Written by

Hermione Redshaw

KidHaven
PUBLISHING

Published in 2023 by **KidHaven Publishing,
an Imprint of Greenhaven Publishing, LLC**
2544 Clinton St., Buffalo, NY 14224

© 2022 Booklife Publishing
This edition is published by arrangement with
Booklife Publishing

Written by: Hermione Redshaw
Edited by: William Anthony
Illustrated by: Amy Li

Font (cover, page 1) courtesy of cuppuccino on
Shutterstock.com. With thanks to Getty Images,
Thinkstock Photo and iStockphoto.

Cataloging-in-Publication Data

Names: Redshaw, Hermione, author. l Li, Amy,
illustrator.
Title: Colors in my world / by Hermione Redshaw,
illustrated by Amy Li.
Description: New York : KidHaven Publishing, 2023.
l Series: The world around me
Identifiers: ISBN 9781534543263 (pbk.) l
ISBN 9781534543287 (library bound) l
ISBN 9781534543294 (ebook)
Subjects: LCSH: Colors--Juvenile literature.
Classification: LCC QC495.5 R394 2023 l
DDC 535.6--dc23

All rights reserved. No part of this book
may be reproduced in any form without
permission in writing from the publisher,
except by a reviewer.

Manufactured in the United States of America

CPSIA compliance information: Batch #CWKH23
For further information contact Greenhaven Publishing LLC
at 1-844-317-7404.

Please visit our website, www.greenhavenpublishing.com.
For a free color catalog of all our high-quality books,
call toll free 1-844-317-7404 or fax 1-844-317-7405.

Find us on

Zoe knows all about colors!
She sees colors everywhere.

Zoe likes 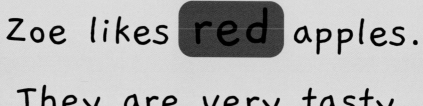 apples.
They are very tasty.

The roses in the garden are red.

Oranges are **orange**.

The fruit and the color
have the same name!

Traffic cones are orange.

They keep people safe.

The rubber duck in the bath is yellow.

Eggs are yellow in the middle.

Zoe likes the yellow part the most.

The grass outside is **green**.
Leaves can be green, too.

Some vegetables are green.

Zoe does not like green vegetables!

The car is **blue**.

Zoe likes blue cars.

There are blue

cushions on the sofa.

Grapes can be purple.

Grapes grow
in bunches.

A butterfly sits on Zoe's nose.

It is purple.

Zoe's favorite ice cream is **pink**.

It tastes like bubble gum!

Flamingos
are pink.

They sometimes
stand on one leg.

Chocolate is brown.

Zoe loves chocolate!

Muddy puddles are
fun to splash in.

Mud is brown.

Zoe has won medals in sports.
Some medals are gold.

The pans in the kitchen are silver.

Silver is shiny.

White is the lightest color.

Zoe's socks are white.

Black is the darkest color.

Zoe's shoes are black.

Zoe's favorite color is green!

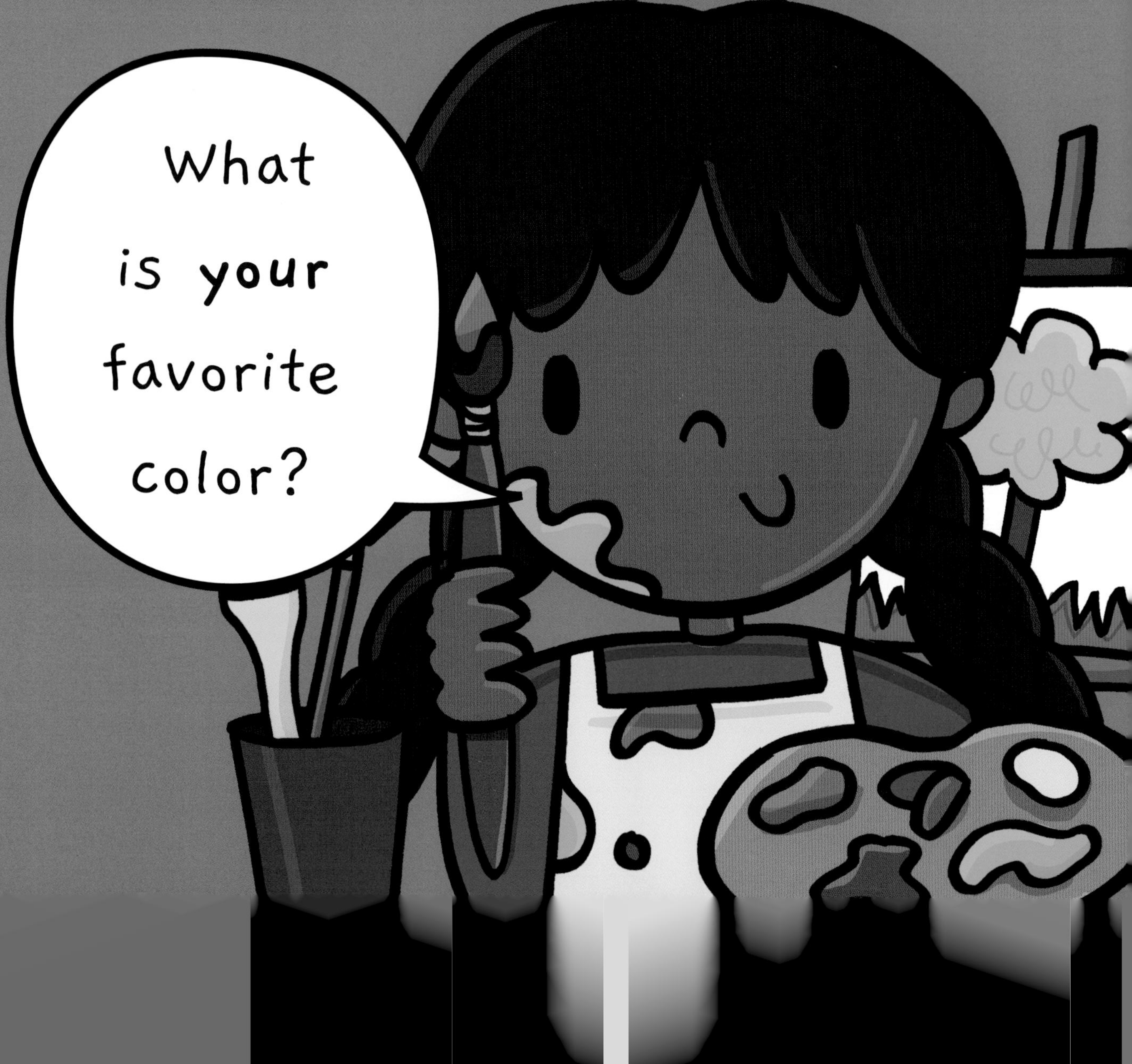